# Stratford-upon-Avon
*Travel Guide*

*Quick Trips Series*

No part of this publication may be reproduced, stored in a retrieval system, or transmitted, in any form or by any means without the prior written permission of the publisher, nor be otherwise circulated in any form of binding or cover other than that in which it is published and without similar condition being imposed on the subsequent purchaser. If there are any errors or omissions in copyright acknowledgements the publisher will be pleased to insert the appropriate acknowledgement in any subsequent printing of this publication. Although we have taken all reasonable care in researching this book we make no warranty about the accuracy or completeness of its content and disclaim all liability arising from its use.

Copyright © 2016, Astute Press
All Rights Reserved.

# Table of Contents

## STRATFORD-UPON-AVON — 6
- Customs & Culture ......... 8
- Geography ......... 9
- Weather & Best Time to Visit ......... 11

## SIGHTS & ACTIVITIES: WHAT TO SEE & DO — 13
- Shakespeare Birthplace Trust ......... 13
- Shakespeare's Homes ......... 15
- Holy Trinity Church ......... 21
- Tudor World Museum & the Falstaff Experience ......... 23
- Royal Shakespeare Company (RSC) ......... 25
- Mechanical Art & Design (MAD) Museum ......... 28
- Stratford Armouries & Wellington Aviation Museum ......... 29
- River Avon Boat Ride ......... 30
- Festivals ......... 32
- Warwick Castle ......... 35

## BUDGET TIPS — 39
- Accommodation ......... 39

**STRATFORD-UPON-AVON TRAVEL GUIDE**

# Stratford-upon-Avon

Stratford-upon-Avon in Warwickshire is a historic town on the river Avon. It is well known as the birthplace of the English playwright and poet, William Shakespeare. Today, Stratford-upon-Avon is the home of the Royal Shakespeare Company (RSC) and their riverside theatre. It is a major tourist destination in the United Kingdom.

# STRATFORD-UPON-AVON TRAVEL GUIDE

Stratford is proud of its Shakespeare heritage and has gone to great lengths to preserve his legacy. Scholars, academics, actors, readers and theatregoers enjoy spending time in the quaint town where he grew up and retired. It's a town he returned to frequently during his adult life (most of which was spent in London) and is the town where he lived out his final years. Shakespeare's enduring legacy is in the words he wrote (all 884,647 of them!)

Stratford-upon-Avon is a town that is remarkably well preserved, due in no small part to Shakespeare's popularity through the centuries (and to its citizens' resourcefulness and ability to recognize the significance of the treasures that are located there). It's home to the Royal Shakespeare Company (RSC), one of the finest theatre companies that regularly perform Shakespeare's plays.

Small though the population may be, Stratford is comprised of warm and welcoming people who have seen to it that Stratford is more than just a museum town. It's a town that has many fine cafes, pubs, restaurants, and shops, and it's a great place to be based to explore the county of Warwickshire.

## 🌎 Customs & Culture

There has been a permanent settlement in Stratford since at least the Anglo-Saxon era and it grew into a prominent medieval market town. It received its charter in 1196 and has existed as an incorporated town for over 800 years. *Strat* is Old English for *street,* and *ford* comes to us unchanged from Old English, indicating that the town

# STRATFORD-UPON-AVON TRAVEL GUIDE

marked the place where a street – likely a Roman road – crossed the Avon.

It was in the mid-18th century when one of the most popular actor's of the day, David Garrick, hosted a three-day Shakespeare festival in Stratford that marked the beginning of what came to be known as "Bardolatry" – defined as the worship (sometimes excessive) of William Shakespeare – and pinned Stratford forevermore onto the tourism map.

After Garrick's festival, performances of Shakespeare's plays became a regular feature in Stratford. That's still the case today: thousands of theatregoers take in a Shakespeare show every week in Stratford. The Royal Shakespeare Company stages dozens of productions each year, so there's always a reason to stay a few days

**STRATFORD-UPON-AVON TRAVEL GUIDE**

to take them all in – and there's always a reason to come back for more.

Tourism and hospitality are the main engines of the Stratford economy, but they aren't the only source of the town's income. Boatbuilding, bicycle manufacture, farming, IT and service sector work are also important to the local economy. Stratford has celebrated its local tradesmen for hundreds of years with an annual "Mop Fair" (see "Festivals" section below).

## 🌍 Geography

Stratford is in the county of Warwickshire in the West Midlands. It is close to the Cotswolds and used to share a tighter relationship with that region (Stratford's textile industry processed the wool of the Cotswolds' sheep until the 19th century).

# **STRATFORD-UPON-AVON TRAVEL GUIDE**

If you plan to travel to Stratford by car, you'll need to get off on Junction 15 of the M40 motorway (from London, this is approximately two hours). It is also easily accessible by rail, and the railway station is just a short walk from the town center.

If you're traveling by plane, Birmingham or East Midlands airports are the closest. From there you can travel by rail or by coach bus.

Within Stratford itself, it's easy to get around on foot. Henley Street, although not the town centre exactly, is the site of Shakespeare's birthplace and is thus a kind of central focal point. Sheep Street is hailed as the restaurant centre of town – appropriate, perhaps, since this was where the sheep butchers were all located until

## STRATFORD-UPON-AVON TRAVEL GUIDE

the late 1800s. Waterside and Southern Lane run along the Avon and are where you will find all of the RSC theatres.

Although you won't need anything more than a comfortable pair of shoes to get you around, you might want to consider hiring a bicycle. The Stratford Greenway provides 5 miles of uninterrupted cycle track. It's located at the edge of town and will take you out into a bit of the Warwickshire countryside.

## 🌍 Weather & Best Time to Visit

Stratford's climate is similar to that of most parts of the British Isles: a temperate maritime climate that is seldom too hot or too cold, but quite often cloudy. Summer highs are typically around 22°C (72°F) with lows of about 10°C

## STRATFORD-UPON-AVON TRAVEL GUIDE

(51°F). Winter temperatures average between highs of around 7°C (44°F) and lows that hover around freezing.

Because the biggest draws for most tourists are the Shakespeare properties and the theatre, there really isn't a bad time to visit: the properties are open all year and there is always something playing at the theatre.

If your schedule is fairly flexible, you might want to see what's on at the RSC and plan your visit around the shows that most interest you. There are also a number of festivals throughout the year (listed under the Sightseeing Highlights section below) that might pique your interest.

**STRATFORD-UPON-AVON TRAVEL GUIDE**

## Sights & Activities: What to See & Do

## Shakespeare Birthplace Trust

The Shakespeare Centre, Henley Street

Tel: 01789 201813

http://www.shakespeare.org.uk/home.html

# **STRATFORD-UPON-AVON TRAVEL GUIDE**

This is this place to begin your sojourn with the Bard. The Shakespeare Birthplace Trust (SBT) was founded in 1847.

That was the year that Shakespeare's birthplace was purchased for conservation purposes. In fact, the SBT is the UK's oldest conservation society and is said to be the most important Shakespeare charity in the world. It receives no funding from the government, so it depends on visitors like you to help maintain all the local Shakespeare properties (about which, more below).

The SBT's current home is in a modern building (built in 1964) adjacent to the birthplace. It's a great place to start your visit because, for one thing, you can buy tickets to all the houses here, but also because the centre itself is a site for excellent exhibitions. The Shakespeare's

### STRATFORD-UPON-AVON TRAVEL GUIDE

Treasure's exhibition displays the playwright's letters and personal effects, as well as props and memorabilia from productions throughout the centuries. Items on display change every six months, so there's always a reason to return.

If you are already a devotee of the Bard, or if your time in Stratford has piqued your interest, the SBT runs an excellent bookshop that is a terrific resource for scholars and the newly curious alike.

## Shakespeare's Homes

At the risk of making an understatement, Shakespeare's body of work is so massive that his legacy easily exists on his writing alone. But it certainly doesn't hurt his international renown that he also left behind quite a bit of property that has attracted visitors from around the world

## STRATFORD-UPON-AVON TRAVEL GUIDE

for over 250 years. A walk through his properties – and those of his relatives – allows you to feel a closeness to their time that makes reading his works or watching a production of his plays feel somehow more current.

The first of these is, of course, his birthplace. It was here, in 1564, that the glove maker's son entered into a world that he would observe and study, and eventually recreate on stage. In these rooms Shakespeare would have experienced the instability brought on by his father's mismanagement of family funds. He would dream, along with his father, of possessing a coat of arms and therefore being someone important – like his mother's relatives, the Ardens, were. He would have felt the religious tension of the times that may have honed his ability for portraying social unrest with painful reality. And while looking out of his window he might have even seen, for the very first

# STRATFORD-UPON-AVON TRAVEL GUIDE

time, troupes of traveling players visiting Stratford to perform mummers shows and plays – a sight that, wherever it may have occurred, must have had a profound effect on the young boy.

After many years as a successful London playwright, Shakespeare was able to afford a property of his own (as well as the coat of arms he dreamt of as a boy). This property was called New Place (a name that's straight to the point and charmingly prosaic, considering the owner's poetic magnitude). During his day, New Place was the second largest home in Stratford. It was here on his birthday in 1616 that Shakespeare died.

Today only the foundations of New Place exist, and, interestingly, Shakespeare was indirectly involved in the house's demise. In the mid-18th century the house was

## STRATFORD-UPON-AVON TRAVEL GUIDE

already a place of pilgrimage for Shakespeare's fans, but its current occupant grew tired of the constant noisy presence of adoring devotees. He took out his frustration on a mulberry tree said to have been planted by Shakespeare. He uprooted it, and the townspeople were aghast – so they broke New Place's windows.

A few years later when the current occupant wished to extend the gardens, his application was denied on account of the Shakespearean relevance of the property. Furious, he demolished the house in 1759 and was swiftly run out of town.

Ironically, the house's foundation is the site of a beautiful garden today, as well as an archaeological dig where many interesting Tudor era artefacts have been unearthed. Next door to New Place was Nash's House

## STRATFORD-UPON-AVON TRAVEL GUIDE

history museum, with farmworkers who run the place as authentically "Tudor" as possible, from the clothes they wear to the tools they use. There is one thing, however that's not *quite* authentic: it's not really Mary Arden's house.

The SBT found documentation in 2000 that proved the house belonged to the Arden family friend, Adam Palmer. Fortune was kind, however: the SBT also discovered that a property very close to the Palmer farm that they'd acquired in the 1960s was the real Arden farmhouse. So even if the farm you visit today is actually Palmer's Farm, it's *still* authentically Tudor – and the real Arden farm is just a short walk away.

This is a great house to visit if you have kids who aren't old enough to fully appreciate the historical and cultural relevance of the other Shakespeare properties. They might not understand the literary allusions made in the other exhibits, but they'll love the farm animals here and be impressed by the falconry shows. Be sure to check the SBT's website (listed above) to see their current programme offerings for children.

The final property of note is Hall's Croft, home of Shakespeare's eldest daughter, Susanna, and her husband, Dr. John Hall. In addition to the period furniture and paintings, this property features texts, utensils and other artefacts concerning 17th century medical practice – some of them from Dr. Hall's personal collection.

## 🌍 Holy Trinity Church

Once you've visited the homes associated with Shakespeare, it's time to visit his final resting place at

# STRATFORD-UPON-AVON TRAVEL GUIDE

Holy Trinity. Parts of the church date back to the 13th century, making it the oldest building in Stratford. Shakespeare was baptized here and was buried inside. His wife, Anne, and daughter, Susanna, were later buried alongside him. The presence of the Shakespeare family has made this the most visited parish church in the England with over 200,000 visitors each year.

Shakespeare's grave is marked by his famous funerary monument. It features a colorful bust and poetic text that proclaims him the equal to Socrates, Virgil and Nestor – and names Mt. Olympus, the seat of the Greek gods, as his final resting place!

Beneath it on the grave itself, an epitaph warns the reader that the person who tries to move the Bard's bones will be cursed. This has fueled the brains of conspiracy theorists

## STRATFORD-UPON-AVON TRAVEL GUIDE

for centuries. Those who believe that the man called William Shakespeare of Stratford and the writer called Shakespeare are not one and the same have longed to exhume his remains. Their belief is that the curse was put in place because his coffin or remains will provide some evidence that he is not who he claimed to be.

The conspiracy theorists aren't the only ones who wish to exhume him. Scientists and historians would like to use modern science to determine his exact cause of death *and* learn if he was a regular marijuana smoker. This particular questions arose from the archaeological dig at New Place which turned up pipes with traces of cannabis.

But conspiracists, historians, scientists and enthusiastic stoners alike have been stymied by that epitaph with its curse. So have those who wished to move his remains to

Westminster Abbey where he'd be in the company of kings and queens.

In truth, it's more than a curse that keeps him from being exhumed: his remains lay beneath the remains of others, and exhumation requires the permission of living descendants. Too many people would need to sign off on the project for it to be feasible. So some questions will need to remain unanswered for now.

# 🌐 Tudor World Museum & the Falstaff Experience

The Shrieves House Barn

40 Sheep Street

Tel: 01789 298070

http://www.falstaffexperience.co.uk/

# STRATFORD-UPON-AVON TRAVEL GUIDE

Whereas the Shakespeare properties inform the visitor of the life of the Bard, his family and his hometown, this lively museum will fill you in on the Tudor world at large.

In the style of a Victorian museum, this maze-like exhibition introduces you to some of the more gruesome aspects of the time: the plague, bear baiting, $16^{th}$ century medical practices, and punishment. Gory themes aside, it's subdued enough that you can bring the kids – who are certain to love it.

The museum also offers a series of themed walks. One of their most popular is their lantern-lit ghostwalk. The museum is said to be one of the most haunted houses in England – so haunted, in fact, that the ghostwalk doesn't permit children, although they now run a family-friendly version of the walk as well.

# STRATFORD-UPON-AVON TRAVEL GUIDE

You can also walk the streets of Stratford with a Shakespeare lookalike if you like. "Shakespeare," dressed in full Elizabethan garb, will lead you through the town and point out all the nooks and crannies that were relevant to his life. This is a particularly fun way to orient yourself and get familiar with the lay of the land.

## 🌐 Royal Shakespeare Company (RSC)

http://www.rsc.org.uk/

A visit to Stratford is simply not complete without attending at least one performance by the Royal Shakespeare Company (RSC). The RSC has been the world's pre-eminent Shakespeare ensemble for over 50 years.

# **STRATFORD-UPON-AVON TRAVEL GUIDE**

In any given season, they will have several productions in rotation here in Stratford, one or two in London, and touring productions that bring the magic of a live, superbly acted Shakespeare production to theatres across the globe.

Shakespeare productions have been a constant feature in Stratford since the 18th century, but it wasn't until 1961 that the RSC established a permanent company in the town and put in on the map in terms of modern theatrical relevance. Thanks to the RSC, Stratford is one of the most important theatre districts in the English-speaking world (after Broadway and the West End, perhaps, but arguably before just about anywhere else).

# STRATFORD-UPON-AVON TRAVEL GUIDE

The RSC runs several different performance spaces, each showcasing different types of plays. The Royal Shakespeare Theatre (RST) is the largest space. It reopened in 2010 after three years of renovations that converted the proscenium stage into a thrust stage that allows the audience to sit around three sides – just as they did in Shakespeare's Globe and other Elizbethan theatres. It can seat 1,040 audience members; given this capacity, this is where the "blockbuster" plays will often be staged.

The Swan Theatre is also a thrust stage, but with seating for only 450 people, it's less than half the size than the RST and therefore provides a large degree of intimacy between the actors and the audience – who are all clearly visible to the players on the stage.

# **STRATFORD-UPON-AVON TRAVEL GUIDE**

The Other Place was a favorite among theatregoers for many years. This black-box theatre featured more avant-garde, fringe performances than its counterparts at the RST and Swan. During the renovation of the other two, however, The Other Place was transformed into the more traditional Courtyard Theatre so that RSC performances could continue within Stratford. Now that the RST and Swan are fully operational again there are plans to revert the Courtyard back into The Other Place.

Although the RSC is the dominant theatre company in the area, it isn't the only one. If you'd like to take in a show that's a bit more light-hearted, you ought to consider seeing a show by the Tread the Boards theatre company at their home in the Attic Theatre. This group also features the occasional Shakespeare production, but tends to offer works by more contemporary playwrights.

While there, be sure to have a drink at the Lazy Cow and enjoy the view of the Avon.

# Mechanical Art & Design (MAD) Museum

Sheep Street

Tel: 01789 2269356

http://themadmuseum.co.uk/

And now for something completely different! Make no mistake: visitors to Stratford can completely immerse themselves in the vast wealth of Shakespearean productions and properties, legends and lore, and have a perfectly satisfying time of it. But there's more to experience here than just Hamlet, Lear and Othello.

**STRATFORD-UPON-AVON TRAVEL GUIDE**

For starters, there's the MAD Museum. This museum showcases the wacky and wonderful in the world of Mechanical Art and Design (aka, MAD) with a particular focus on kinetic art (that is to say, artwork that has moving parts). From works made of Legos and an Erector sets to animatronic dinosaurs, Rube Goldberg contraptions and beyond, this is a museum designed with a great sense of whimsy and fun. With plenty of buttons to push and levers to pull, the MAD Museum is sure to delight visitors of all ages.

# 🌍 Stratford Armouries & Wellington Aviation Museum

Gospel Oak Lane

Tel: 01789 262468

http://www.stratfordarmouries.com/

http://www.wellingtonaviation.org/

# STRATFORD-UPON-AVON TRAVEL GUIDE

This museum exhibits nearly 700 years of arms and armour. Collection highlights include a life-sized Indian elephant in full battle gear (built by Terry English, armourer for the Harry Potter films), a Latanka cannon from 1450 which is believed to be the oldest cannon on display anywhere, and a crossbow built according to plans drawn up by Leonardo Da Vinci. This latter piece is quite a spectacle. With arms that measure 80 feet, this is not your modern hunter's crossbow. It is more like an early cannon, in fact, and the team that built it wanted to see if Leonardo's plans were truly workable or if it was more of a playful sketch dreamed up in the genius's brain.

The Stratford Armouries have recently become the home to the Wellington Aviation Museum (previously located in Gloucestershire). This collection features Royal Air Force

**STRATFORD-UPON-AVON TRAVEL GUIDE**

memorabilia from WWII. You'll find decommissioned bomber planes, bomb cases, equipment, uniforms and other examples of weaponry from the era. The museum housed on RAF Snitterfield, a former air station located just to the north of Stratford.

# River Avon Boat Ride

**Bancroft Cruises**

Holiday Inn Stratford

Bridgefoot

Tel: 01789 269669

http://www.bancroftcruisers.co.uk/

**Avon Boating Limited**

Swan's Nest Way

Tel: 01789 267073

# STRATFORD-UPON-AVON TRAVEL GUIDE

http://www.avon-boating.co.uk/

The town is often referred to simply as *Stratford*, but it's worth remembering that its full name includes *–upon-Avon*. Although Shakespeare takes center stage in terms of Stratford's tourism, the River Avon and its canal flow serenely through the town and are worth some of your time.

An excellent way to experience the river is on a boat cruise, and there are several excellent companies that provide river tours. Not only will you experience the Shakespearean sites you've already seen, like the Royal Shakespeare Theatre and Holy Trinity Church, from the vantage point of the water, but you'll also enjoy the beauty of the Warwickshire countryside.

# STRATFORD-UPON-AVON TRAVEL GUIDE

Bancroft Cruises offers 45-minute tours that are especially popular for the cream teas they serve during your ride. The company offers special discounts online from time to time through Living Social, so check out that website, but even without a discount adults ride for £5.50.

Avon Boating offers similar tours at the same price, but differentiates itself through its partnership with The Bear pub and the Bistrot Pierre. If you're traveling with a group (minimum of 12), you can book one of their several cruise and meal packages.

Avon Boating also has rowboats and punts for hire by the hour. This is an excellent way to see the river at your own speed (and a great workout to boot!).

# STRATFORD-UPON-AVON TRAVEL GUIDE

## 🌍 Festivals

Throughout the year, Stratford hosts some wonderful festivals. Since the anniversary of Shakespeare's birth and death falls on 23 April, you can bet that month is high season for Shakespeare celebration.

Sure enough, his birthday has been caused for public celebration for over 200 years, complete with a parade of costumed revelers, street performers, vendors of all sorts – and a communal singing of "Happy Birthday" to the Bard (http://www.shakespearesbirthday.org.uk/). If parades are a bit too slow for you, you might want to sign up for the Shakespeare Marathon, also held in April (http://www.shakespearemarathon.org.uk/).

The last week of May and into June is when the Stratford-upon-Avon Arts Festival takes place. This is an incredibly

## STRATFORD-UPON-AVON TRAVEL GUIDE

comprehensive week for all the arts. There is a busy roundup of fringe theatre performances, stand-up comedy and music; there is a fun and funky film festival and exhibitions of visual artists. It's an engaging week, and a lot of fun.

(http://www.stratforduponavonartsfestival.co.uk/)


For one weekend in the summer (sometimes June, sometimes July) all of Stratford heads to the banks of the river for the River Festival. This is a time to celebrate the Avon's boats (including a boat parade!), local arts and crafts, live music and an excellent display of fireworks.

(http://www.stratfordriverfestival.co.uk/)


On Sundays from May through early September, head to the Stratford Bandstand to hear a variety of horn, swing

## STRATFORD-UPON-AVON TRAVEL GUIDE

and jazz ensembles. They'll have your toes tapping in no time.

September is the time for the Stratford Food Festival. During this event, you can attend talks and master classes from some of the UK's most popular chefs, celebrate Britain's brewers at the Real Ale bar, attend cookbook signings, hear some live music – and of course come away with some amazing high-quality ingredients for all the new recipes you've learned. It's held at the Stratford Racecourse (which is also the place to go, incidentally, if you're into horse races). (http://www.stratfordfoodfestival.co.uk/)

If it's October, it's time for the Mop Fair. "What's a mop fair?" you ask. Five hundred years ago it was a means for skilled laborers to meet with new employers – a kind of

**STRATFORD-UPON-AVON TRAVEL GUIDE**

hiring fair held every October. Workers paraded about holding symbols of their trade – and those whose trade or skill had no discernible symbol would carry mops. Once the workers were hired, however, it became a time of celebration, and today it retains more of that character. It is still the case today as it was then that the fair takes over the entire town centre, so it's a time of rollicking good fun throughout Stratford.

## 🌐 Warwick Castle

http://www.warwick-castle.com/

Just up the River Avon from Stratford you'll come across Warwick Castle. It's so close to Stratford – and so enchanting – that you'll want to make it part of your trip.

# STRATFORD-UPON-AVON TRAVEL GUIDE

The British Tourist Authority named Warwick Castle one of the "top ten historic houses and monuments" in Britain (a list that also included Stonehenge and the Tower of London – just to give you a sense of its magnificence). Additionally, the *Good Britain Guide 2003* deemed it the UK's best castle.

There has been a castle on this spot since the early days of the Norman Conquest when William the Conqueror himself saw a need for fortifications to keep control of the midlands. Originally a wooden structure, the fortress was replaced by a stone fortress in the 12th century. Every century saw more additions to the castle, but unlike many others it never found itself in ruins. Rather, it has stood witness to all the major events in British and world history of the last 1000 years. Richard III added towers to it, Elizabeth I stayed for a visit. James I gave it to Fulke

# STRATFORD-UPON-AVON TRAVEL GUIDE

Greville who converted it into a country house and is said to haunt its ramparts at night.

The Grevilles opened the property up to tourism in the late 17th century, so it has been entertaining visitors with its picturesque towers and fairy tale façade for over 300 years. In the 1970s, after 374 years of residence, the Grevilles ushered in a whole new era of tourism when they moved out and sold the castle to Tussaud's Group, now owned by Merlin Entertainments, a leisure and amusement company second in the world to Disney.

Today when you visit, you'll enjoy a variety of living history reenactments – the summer jousts are particularly popular. Kids will love the Horrible Histories performances that recreate five eras of history – from the

"Terrible Tudors" to the "Vile Victorians" – in entertainingly gruesome ways.

A walk through the castle itself will take you through a variety of historical settings painstakingly recreated by the artists of Madame Tussauds. The Kingmaker exhibit walks you through the story of the 15$^{th}$ century battle that earned Richard Neville the Earldom of Warwick. The Royal Weekend exhibit will give you a glimpse of how Victorian aristocrats might have experienced the castle. The Castle Dungeon – in addition to being eerie in and of itself – now includes an exhibit recalling the accusation, arrest and punishment of a local woman who was thought to be a witch (children under 10 not admitted).

## **STRATFORD-UPON-AVON TRAVEL GUIDE**

In addition to all of this, there is an ever-changing assortment of events throughout the year, so be sure to check out the castle's website for the latest offerings.

**STRATFORD-UPON-AVON TRAVEL GUIDE**

Budget Tips

## Accommodation

## Premier Inn Central

Payton Street

Tel: 08715 279282

http://www.premierinn.com/en/hotel/STUPAV/stratford-upon-avon-central

**STRATFORD-UPON-AVON TRAVEL GUIDE**

# Premier Inn, Stratford-upon-Avon Waterways

The Waterways, Birmingham Road

Tel: 08715 279316

http://www.premierinn.com/en/hotel/STRAVO/stratford-upon-avon-waterways

The Premier Inn has built its reputation for reliably providing excellent comfort at a price that won't make you sweat.

Rooms start at £29 and amenities include free WiFi, television that features 80 channels, a coffee maker, a hair dryer and blackout curtains to keep the morning sunlight out of your eyes. Their Thyme restaurant provides breakfast and a menu of traditional and contemporary options throughout the day.

# STRATFORD-UPON-AVON TRAVEL GUIDE

# Mercure Stratford-upon-Avon Shakespeare Hotel

Chapel Street

Tel: 08456 200900

http://www.accorhotels.com/gb/hotel-6630-mercure-stratford-upon-avon-shakespeare-hotel/room.shtml

This hotel will amplify your total Shakespeare experience. The building is over 400 years old, but renovations have made, of course, so you can experience a step back in time with the modern conveniences that you expect in a 21st century hotel stay.

It is centrally located, particularly close to the RSC theatres. All rooms are individualized in theme and décor (and each has a different name) but all include the following amenities: WiFi, en suite toilet, air conditioners,

**STRATFORD-UPON-AVON TRAVEL GUIDE**

television, coffee and tea making facilities, hair dryer. Rates start at £79, but there are excellent deals to be found online.

## Best Western Grosvenor Hotel

Warwick Road

Tel: 08457 767676

http://www.bestwestern.co.uk/hotels/grosvenor-hotel-stratford-upon-avon-83851/hotel-info/default.aspx

Best Western has an international reputation for simple comfort at affordable prices, and this location is no different. Clean, cosy and located in the midst of everything, you'll be an easy walk from all theatres and Shakespeare properties. Amenities include free internet, television, hair dryer, coffee and tea maker, and also include a convenient laptop-sized safe. Rates booked through their website start at £89, but online deals can be found for under £70.

# Legacy Falcon Hotel

Chapel Street

Tel: 08444 119005

http://www.legacy-hotels.co.uk/legacy-thefalcon/home.asp

If you're looking for a hotel with local character as well as an affordable price, check out the Legacy Falcon Hotel.

Outside it looks like a 16$^{th}$ century pub (which it may well have been), but the renovations inside have been done with care and good taste in order to modernise without removing all traces of the building's original charm. Rooms come equipped with free broadband internet connection (there is free WiFi in the bar and lounge), en

## STRATFORD-UPON-AVON TRAVEL GUIDE

suite toilet, hair dryer, television with pay-per-view movies, tea and coffee making facilities. Online discounted rates can be found for under £70.

# Travelodge Stratford-upon-Avon

261 Birmingham Road

tel: 08719 846414

http://www.travelodge.co.uk/hotels/376/Stratford-Upon-Avon-hotel

This hotel is about a mile the train station and just over a mile from the Shakespeare Birthplace Trust and RSC theatres.

It may require a short cab ride after a night at the theatre, but with rates starting at £46, the Travelodge is a dependable good deal. Amenities include en suite toilet/shower, WiFi (for a small fee), coffee and tea making facilities. The hotel does not include air-conditioning, not usually a problem in Great Britain.

## 🌎 Places to Eat

## Loxleys Restaurant & Wine Bar

3 Sheep Street

Tel: 01789 292128

http://www.loxleysrestaurant.co.uk/

Loxleys used to be a clothing retailer that served Stratford for many decades. When the shop went out of business, the new owners of the property kept the name but converted the space into the elegant wine bar and restaurant that exists there today. Their menu is seasonal and produced with the finest local ingredients. The cuisine is a mixture of Italian and modern British fare. Main courses range between £10-17, with steaks being a bit more.

# Bamboodle

7-9 Union Street

Tel: 01789 414999

http://www.bamboodle.co.uk/

Bamboodle bills itself as an Asian street-food tapas bar. They offer an assortment of South Asian curries, noodle bowls, and meat and poultry boards, as well as an assortment of tapas-sized bites.

The serving staff is both friendly and knowledgeable – especially when it comes to pairing drinks with your meal. Although they offer the option of purchasing a whole crispy duck for £28, the majority of items on the menu are under £10.

# Spoonfuls

10-11-12 Shrieves Walk

Tel: 01789 267753

http://www.spoonfuls.co.uk/

Tucked away in an alley that connects Sheep Street and Bridge Street is Spoonfuls, a hidden gem of a cafe. By day, it's a traditional British tea shop; by night it becomes a delicious Southern Indian restaurant – so you do need to decide which kind of fare you're in the mood for so that you know when to show up. From steak to smoothies, cream tea to curry, they have it all – and at prices that are incredibly reasonable. A couple can have an entrée and a glass of wine for less than £20.

**STRATFORD-UPON-AVON TRAVEL GUIDE**

# Lambs of Sheep Street

12 Sheep Street

tel: 01789 292554

http://www.lambsrestaurant.co.uk/

This location – one of the oldest buildings in Stratford – just begs for a romantic dinner with its Tudor exterior and exposed 16$^{th}$ century wooden beams along the ceiling inside.

The old is a fine compliment to the new in this otherwise completely modern, warmly decorated restaurant. The cuisine is predominantly British, traditional with some experimentation, but always using the finest local ingredients. Their wine list is extensive and they'll be happy to help you pair your glass and plate. Most entrees are less than £17, which is also the price of their three course prix-fixe meal if you happen to stop by for lunch.

# El Greco

27 Rother Street

tel: 01789 290505

http://www.el-greco.co.uk/

El Greco, as the name may have given away, is a Greek restaurant. It's come to be a local favorite, and no surprise. The food is delicious and incredibly colorful, the ambience is lively and fun.

If you're familiar with Greek food, you'll find exactly what you're looking for. If it's new to you, don't worry – the staff is welcoming and ready to match something to your tastes. In fact, those who first experienced Greek food at

El Greco have been some of its most enthusiastic cheerleaders. Main courses range between £12-17.

# 🌏 Shopping

## Shakespeare Gift Shops

Located at each of the Shakespeare properties, the SBT operates many shops dedicated to the town's favorite son. Here you'll find every play by Shakespeare and a large number of the biographies and teaching resources that are out there. But in addition to the serious scholarship, you'll also be struck by all the light-hearted keepsakes. From witty t-shirts, magnets and toiletries, to Shakespeare rubber ducks, teddy bears and finger puppets, you'll find everything Shakespeare you could ever have wished for…and then some.

**STRATFORD-UPON-AVON TRAVEL GUIDE**

# Chaucer Head Bookshop

21 Chapel Street

Tel: 01789 415691

http://www.chaucerhead.com/

Chances are, if you've spent enough time in Stratford you've got books on your mind. Come and satisfy your bibliophile needs at the Chaucer Head.

Of their 12,000 secondhand tomes, you'll find (of course) plenty of writing by and about Shakespeare, as well as the shop's namesake, Jane Austen, the Brontes, and all the greats of the English canon. You'll also find a good selection of local and regional history books.

# STRATFORD-UPON-AVON TRAVEL GUIDE

# Much Ado About Toys

The Old Bus Depot

Guild Street

Tel: 01789 295850

This is more than just a toy shop: it's a labor of love. This shop has been family-run since the 1990s, and you'll enjoy the assortment of antique and collectible toys they've assembled. This is a must-see for fans of toy trains and radio controlled cars and trucks because the name is more than just a play on Shakespeare: there really *is* a lot of 'ado' that's gone into this shop. Whether you walk away toting bags or empty-handed, you'll be glad you visited.

# Department Stores

You won't have to wander far to realize that Stratford is actually quite an excellent town for shopping. Its visitors can enjoy many hours exploring its boutiques and smaller franchises located all around the town center. But if you find yourself without much time to shop around and in need of someplace familiar that you can navigate quickly, you needn't go much further than Marks & Spencer or Debenhams. M&S is located at 29-30 Bridge Street, and Debenhams is 3-4 Wood Street.

# Henley Street Treats & Sweets

# Benson's House of Tea

33 Henley Street

Tel: 01789 296996

http://www.bensonshouseoftea.com/

**STRATFORD-UPON-AVON TRAVEL GUIDE**

# Truffles Chocolatier

48 Henley Street

Tel: 01789 267555

http://www.truffles-chocolatier.co.uk/

After your visit to Shakespeare's Birthplace on Henley Street, you might find yourself wanting a tea and something sweet. Benson's House of Tea is a specialist in loose teas from all over the world. Their selection is so large it might be difficult to make a decision; this being Stratford, why not go with the Bard's Brew, their house blend? Then walk down the street to Truffles Chocolatier and try some of their handmade English chocolates. The owners also run the Little Sweet Shop that specializes in old time candies that those of a certain vintage will remember from their childhood.

# STRATFORD-UPON-AVON TRAVEL GUIDE

# STRATFORD-UPON-AVON TRAVEL GUIDE

## 🌎 Entry Requirements

Citizens of the European Union do not need a visa when visiting the UK. Non-EU members from European countries within the European Economic Area (EEA) are also exempt. This includes countries like Iceland, Norway, Liechtenstein and Switzerland. Visitors from Canada, Australia, Japan, Malaysia, Hong Kong SAR, New Zealand, Singapore, South Korea and the USA do not need a visa to visit the UK, provided that their stay does not exceed 6 months. Visitors from Oman, Qatar and the United Arab Emirates may apply for an Electronic Visa Waiver (EVW) via the internet, if their stay in the UK is less than 6 months. You will need a visa to visit the UK, if travelling from India, Jamaica, Cuba, South Africa, Thailand, the People's Republic of China, Saudi Arabia, Zimbabwe, Indonesia, Cambodia, Nigeria, Ghana, Kenya, Egypt, Ethiopia, Vietnam, Turkey, Taiwan, Pakistan, Russia, the Philippines, Iran, Afghanistan and more. If you are in doubt about the status of your country, do inquire with officials of the relevant UK Embassy, who should be able to advise you. Visitors from the EU (European Union) or EEA (European Economic Area) will not require immigration clearance when staying in the Isle of Man, but may require a work permit if they wish to take employment there. If needed, a visa for the Isle of Man may be obtained from the British Embassy or High Commission in your country. Applications can be made via the Internet.

# **STRATFORD-UPON-AVON TRAVEL GUIDE**

If you wish to study in the UK, you will need to qualify for a student visa. There are a number of requirements. First, you have to provide proof of acceptance into an academic institution and available funding for tuition, as well as monthly living costs. A health surcharge of £150 will be levied for access to the National Health Service. Applications can be made online and will be subject to a points based evaluation system.

If you need to visit the UK for professional reasons, there are several different classes of temporary work visas. Charity volunteers, sports professionals and creative individuals can qualify for a stay of up to 12 months, on submission of a certificate of sponsorship. Nationals from Canada, Australia, Japan, Monaco, New Zealand, Hong Kong, Taiwan and the Republic of Korea can also apply for the Youth Mobility Scheme that will allow them to work in the UK for up to two years, if they are between the ages of 18 and 30. Citizens of Commonwealth member countries may qualify for an ancestral visa that will enable them to stay for up to 5 years and apply for an extension.

# STRATFORD-UPON-AVON TRAVEL GUIDE

## Health Insurance

Visitors from the European Union or EEA (European Economic Area) countries are covered for using the UK's National Health Service, by virtue of a European Health Insurance Card (EHIC). This includes visitors from Switzerland, Liechtenstein, the Canary Islands and Iceland. The card can be applied for free of charge. If you are in doubt about the process, the European Commission has created phone apps for Android, IPhone and Windows to inform European travellers about health matters in various different countries.

Bear in mind that a slightly different agreement is in place for Crown Dependencies, such as the Isle of Man and the Channel Islands. There is a reciprocal agreement between the UK and the Isle of Man with regards to basic healthcare, but this does not include the option of repatriation, which could involve a considerable expense, should facilities such as an Air Ambulance be required. If visiting the UK from the Isle of Man, do check the extent of your health insurance before your departure. A similar reciprocal agreement exists between the UK and the Channel Islands. This covers basic emergency healthcare, but it is recommended that you inquire about travel health insurance if visiting the UK from the Channel Islands.

# STRATFORD-UPON-AVON TRAVEL GUIDE

The UK has a reciprocal healthcare agreement with several countries including Australia, New Zealand, Barbados, Gibraltar, the Channel Islands, Montserrat, Romania, Turkey, Switzerland, the British Virgin Islands, the Caicos Islands, Bulgaria, the Falkland Islands and Anguilla, which means that nationals of these countries are covered when visiting the UK. In some cases, only emergency care is exempted from charges. Reciprocal agreements with Armenia, Azerbaijan, Belarus, Georgia, Kazakhstan, Kyrgyzstan, Moldova, Russia, Tajikistan, Turkmenistan, Ukraine and Uzbekistan were terminated at the beginning of 2016 and no longer apply.

Visitors from non European countries without medical insurance will be charged 150 percent of the usual rate, should they need to make use of the National Health Service (NHS). Exemptions exist for a number of categories, including refugees, asylum seekers. Anyone with a British work permit is also covered for health care. Find out the extent of your health cover before leaving home and make arrangements for adequate travel insurance, if you need additional cover.

**Travelling with pets**

If travelling from another country within the EU, your pet will be able to enter the UK without quarantine, provided that

## STRATFORD-UPON-AVON TRAVEL GUIDE

certain entry requirements are met. The animal will need to be microchipped and up to date on rabies vaccinations. This means that the vaccinations should have occurred no later than 21 days before your date of departure. In the case of dogs, treatment against tapeworm must also be undertaken before your departure. You will need to carry an EU pet passport. If travelling from outside the EU, a third-country official veterinary certificate will need to be issued within 10 days of your planned departure. Check with your vet or the UK embassy in your country about specific restrictions or requirements for travel with pets.

In the case of cats travelling from Australia, a statement will need to be issued by the Australian Department of Agriculture to confirm that your pet has not been in contact with carriers of the Hendra virus. If travelling from Malaysia, you will need to carry documentation from a vet that your pet has tested negative for the Nipah virus within 10 days before your departure. There are no restrictions on pet rodents, rabbits, birds, reptilians, fish, amphibians or reptiles, provided that they are brought from another EU country. For pet rabbits and rodents from countries outside the European Union, a four month quarantine period will be required, as well as a rabies import licence. Entry is prohibited for prairie dogs from the USA and squirrels and rodents from sub-Saharan Africa.

# STRATFORD-UPON-AVON TRAVEL GUIDE

# 🌐 Airports, Airlines & Hubs

### Airports

London, the capital of England and the UK's most popular tourist destination is served by no less than 6 different airports. Of these, the best known is **Heathrow International Airport (LHR)**, which ranks as the busiest airport in the UK and Europe and sixth busiest in the world. Heathrow is located about 23km to the west of the central part of London. It is utilized by more than 90 airlines and connects to 170 destinations around the world. The second busiest is **Gatwick Airport (LGW)**, which lies 5km north of Crawley and about 47km south of the central part of London. Its single runway is the world's busiest and in particular, it offers connections to the most popular European destinations. From 2013, it offered travellers a free flight connection service, called Gatwick Connect if the service is not available through their individual airlines. **London Luton Airport (LTN)** is located less than 3km from Luton and about 56km north of London's city center. It is the home of EasyJet, the UK's largest airline, but also serves as a base for Monarch, Thomson Airlines and Ryanair. **London Stansted Airport (STN)** is the fourth busiest airport in the UK. Located about 48km northeast of London, it is an important base for Ryanair and also utilized by EasyJet, Thomas Cook Airline and Thomson Airways. **London Southend Airport (SEN)** is

# STRATFORD-UPON-AVON TRAVEL GUIDE

located in Essex, about 68km from London's central business area. Once the third busiest airport in London, it still handles air traffic for EasyJet and Flybe. Although **City Airport (LCY)** is the nearest to the city center of London, its facilities are compact and limiting. The short runway means that it is not really equipped to handle large aircraft and the airport is not operational at night either. It is located in the Docklands area, about 6.4km from Canary Wharf and mainly serves business travellers. Despite these restrictions, it is still the 5th busiest airport in London and 13th busiest in Europe.

The UK's third busiest airport is **Manchester International Airport (MAN)**, which is located about 13.9km southwest of Manchester's CBD. **Birmingham Airport (BHX)** is located 10km from Birmingham's CBD and offers connections to domestic as well as international destinations. **Newcastle International Airport (NCL)** is located about 9.3km from Newcastle's city center and offers connections to Tyne and Wear, Northumberland, Cumbria, North Yorkshire and even Scotland. **Leeds/Bradford Airport (LBA)** provides connections to various cities in the Yorkshire area, including Leeds, Bradford, York and Wakefield. **Liverpool International Airport (LPL)**, also known as Liverpool John Lennon Airport, serves the north-western part of England and provides connections to destinations in Germany, France, Poland, the Netherlands, Spain, Greece, Cyprus, the USA, the Canary

# STRATFORD-UPON-AVON TRAVEL GUIDE

Islands, Malta, Jersey and the Isle of Man. **Bristol Airport (BRS)** provides international access to the city of Bristol, as well as the counties of Somerset and Gloucestershire. As the 9th busiest airport in the UK, it also serves as a base for budget airlines such as EasyJet and Ryanair. **East Midlands Airport (EMA)** connects travellers to Nottingham.

**Edinburgh Airport (EDI)** is the busiest in Scotland and one of the busier airports in the UK. Its primary connections are to London, Bristol, Birmingham, Belfast, Amsterdam, Paris, Frankfurt, Dublin and Geneva. Facilities include currency exchange, a pet reception center and tourist information desk. **Glasgow International Airport (GLA)** is the second busiest airport in Scotland and one of the 10 busiest airports of the UK. As a gateway to the western part of Scotland, it also serves as a primary airport for trans-Atlantic connections to Scotland and as a base for budget airlines such as Ryanair, Flybe, EasyJet and Thomas Cook. **Cardiff Airport (CWL)** lies about 19km west of the city center of Cardiff and provides access to Cardiff, as well as the south, mid and western parts of Wales. In particular, it offers domestic connections to Glasgow, Edinburgh, Belfast, Aberdeen and Newcastle. **Belfast International Airport (BFS)** is the gateway to Northern Ireland and welcomes approximately 4 million passengers per year. **Kirkwall Airport (KOI)** was originally built for use by the RAF in 1940, but reverted to civilian aviation from 1948. It is located near the town of

# STRATFORD-UPON-AVON TRAVEL GUIDE

Kirkwall and serves as gateway to the Orkney Islands. It is mainly utilized by the regional Flybe service and the Scottish airline, Loganair. The airports at **Guernsey (GCI)** and **Jersey (JER)** offer access to the Channel Islands.

## Airlines

British Airways (BA) is the UK's flag carrier airline and was formed around 1972 from the merger of British Overseas Airways Corporation (BOAC) and British European Airways (BEA). It has the largest fleet in the UK and flies to over 160 destinations on 6 different continents. A subsidiary, BA CityFlyer, manages domestic and European connections. British Airways Limited maintains an executive service linking London to New York. The budget airline EasyJet is based at London Luton Airport. In terms of annual passenger statistics, it is Britain's largest airline and Europe's second largest airline after Ryanair. With 19 bases around Europe, it fosters strong connections with Italy, France, Germany and Spain. Thomas Cook Airlines operates as the air travel division of the Thomas Cook group, Britain and the world's oldest travel agent. Thomson Airways is the world's largest charter airline, resulting from a merger between TUI AG and First Choice Holidays. The brand operates scheduled and chartered flights connecting Ireland and the UK with Europe, Africa, Asia and North

# STRATFORD-UPON-AVON TRAVEL GUIDE

America. Founded in the 1960s, Monarch Airlines still operates under the original brand identity and maintains bases at Leeds, Birmingham, Gatwick and Manchester. Its primary base is at London Luton Airport. Jet2.com is a budget airline based at Leeds/Bradford, which offers connections to 57 destinations. Virgin Atlantic, the 7th largest airline in the UK, operates mainly from its bases at Heathrow, Gatwick and Manchester Airport.

Flybe is a regional, domestic service which provides connections to UK destinations. Covering the Channel Islands, Flybe is in partnership with Blue Islands, an airline based on the island of Guernsey. Blue Islands offers connections from Guernsey to Jersey, London, Southampton, Bristol, Dundee, Zurich and Geneva. Loganair is a regional Scottish airline which is headquartered at Glasgow International Airport. It provides connections to various destinations in Scotland, including Aberdeen, Edinburgh, Inverness, Norwich and Dundee. Additionally it operates a service to the Shetland Islands, the Orkney Islands and the Western Islands in partnership with Flybe. BMI Regional, also known as British Midland Regional Limited, is based at East Midlands Airport and offers connections to other British destinations such as Aberdeen, Bristol and Newcastle, as well as several cities in Europe.

# STRATFORD-UPON-AVON TRAVEL GUIDE

## Hubs

Heathrow Airport serves as a primary hub for British Airways. Gatwick Airport serves as a hub for British Airways and EasyJet. EasyJet is based at London Luton Airport, but also maintains a strong presence at London's Stansted Airport and Bristol Airport. Manchester Airport serves as a hub for the regional budget airline Flybe, as does Birmingham Airport. Thompson Airways maintain bases at three of London's airports, namely Gatwick, London Luton and Stansted, as well as Belfast, Birmingham, Bournemouth, Bristol, Cardiff, Doncaster/Sheffield, East Midlands, Edinburgh, Exeter, Glasgow, Leeds/Bradford, Manchester and Newcastle. Jet2.com has bases at Leeds/Bradford, Belfast, East Midlands, Edinburgh, Glasgow, Manchester and Newcastle. Glasgow International Airport serves as the primary hub for the Scottish airline, Loganair, which also has hubs at Edinburgh, Dundee, Aberdeen and Inverness.

## Sea Ports

As the nearest English port to the French coast, Dover in Kent has been used to facilitate Channel crossings to the European mainland for centuries. This makes it one of the busiest passenger ports in the world. Annually, 16 million passengers,

## STRATFORD-UPON-AVON TRAVEL GUIDE

2.8 million private vehicles and 2.1 million trucks pass through its terminals. Three ferry services to France are based on the Eastern dock, connecting passengers to ports in Calais and Dunkirk. Additionally, the Port of Dover also has a cruise terminal, as well as a marina.

The Port of Southampton is a famous port on the central part of the south coast of the UK. It enjoys a sheltered location thanks to the proximity of the Isle of Wight and a tidal quirk that favours its facilities for bulky freighters as well as large cruise liners. The port serves as a base for several UK cruise operators including Cunard, Celebrity Cruises, P&O Cruises, Princess Cruises and Royal Caribbean. Other tour operators using its terminals include MSC Cruises, Costa Cruises, Crystal Cruises and Fred. Olsen Cruise Lines. Southampton is a popular departure point for various cruises to European cities such as Hamburg, Rotterdam, Amsterdam, Le Havre, Bruges, Barcelona, Lisbon, Genoa and Scandinavia, as well as trans-Atlantic destinations such as Boston, New York and Miami. A short but popular excursion is the two day cruise to Guernsey. Southampton also offers ferry connections to the Isle of Wight and the village of Hythe. The port has four cruise terminals and is well-connected by rail to London and other locations in the UK.

# STRATFORD-UPON-AVON TRAVEL GUIDE

### Eurochannel

The Eurotunnel (or the Channel Tunnel) was completed in 1994 and connects Folkestone in Kent with Coquelles near Calais. This offers travellers a new option for entering the UK from the European continent. Via the Eurostar rail network, passengers travelling to or from the UK are connected with destinations across Europe, including Paris, Brussels, Frankfurt, Amsterdam and Geneva. On the UK side, it connects to the London St Pancras station. Also known as St Pancras International, this station is one of the UK's primary terminals for the Eurostar service. The Eurotunnel Shuttle conveys private and commercial vehicles through the tunnel and provides easy motorway access on either side.

# Money Matters

### Currency

The currency of the UK is the Pound Sterling. Notes are issued in denominations of £5, £10, £20 and £50. Coins are issued in denominations of £2, £1, 50p, 20p, 10p, 5p, 2p and 1p. Regional variants of the pound are issued in Scotland and Northern Ireland, but these are acceptable as legal tender in other parts of the UK as well. The Isles of Jersey, Guernsey and

# STRATFORD-UPON-AVON TRAVEL GUIDE

Man issue their own currency, known respectively as the Jersey Pound, the Guernsey Pound and the Manx Pound. However, the Pound Sterling (and its Scottish and Northern Irish variants) can also be used for payment on the Isle of Man, Jersey and Guernsey.

## Banking/ATMs

ATM machines, also known locally as cashpoints or a hole in the wall, are well distributed in cities and larger towns across the UK. Most of these should be compatible with your own banking network, and may even be enabled to give instructions in multiple languages. A small fee is charged per transaction. Beware of helpful strangers, tampering and other scams at ATM machines. Banking hours vary according to bank group and location, but you can generally expect trading hours between 9.30am and 4.30pm.

## Credit Cards

Credit cards are widely accepted at many businesses in the UK, but you may run into smaller shops, restaurants and pubs that do not offer credit card facilities. Cash is still king in the British pub, although most have adapted to credit card use. For hotel

## STRATFORD-UPON-AVON TRAVEL GUIDE

bookings or car rentals, credit cards are essential. Visa and MasterCard are most commonly used. Acceptance of American Express and Diners Club is less widespread. Chip and PIN cards are the norm in the UK. While shops will generally have card facilities that can still accept older magnetic strip or US chip-and-signature cards, you will find that ticket machines and self service vendors are not configured for those types of credit cards.

**Tourist Tax**

A tourist tax of £1 for London has been under discussion, but to date nothing has been implemented. The areas of Cornwall, Brighton, Edinburgh, Westminster and Birmingham also considered implementing a tourist tax, but eventually rejected the idea.

**Claiming back VAT**

If you are not from the European Union, you can claim back VAT (or Value Added Tax) paid on your purchases in the UK. The VAT rate in the UK is 20 percent, but to qualify for a refund, certain conditions will have to be met. Firstly, VAT can only be claimed merchants participating in a VAT refund program scheme. If this is indicated, you can ask the retailer for a VAT 407 form. You may need to provide proof of eligibility by producing your passport. Customs authorities at your point of departure from the European Union (this could be the UK or another country) will inspect the completed form as well as your purchased goods. You should receive your refund from a refund booth at the airport or from the refund department of the retailer where you bought the goods.

## Tipping Policy

It is customary to tip for taxis, restaurants and in bars where you are served by waiting staff, rather than bartenders. The usual rate is between 10 and 15 percent. Some restaurants will add this automatically to your bill as a service charge, usually at a rate of 12.5 percent. Tipping is not expected in most pubs, although you may offer a small sum (traditionally the price of a half pint), with the words "and have one yourself". Some hotels will also add a service charge of between 10 and 15 percent to your bill. You may leave a tip for room-cleaning staff upon departure. Tip bellboys and porters to express your gratitude for a particular service, such as helping with your luggage or organizing a taxi or booking a tour. Tipping is not expected at fast food, self service or takeaway outlets, but if the food is delivered, do tip the delivery person. You may also tip a tour

## STRATFORD-UPON-AVON TRAVEL GUIDE

guide between £2 and £5 per person, or £1 to £2 if part of a family group, especially if the person was attentive, engaging and knowledgeable. In Scotland, most restaurants do not levy a service charge and it is customary to tip between 10 and 15 percent. Tipping in Scottish pubs is not necessary, unless you were served a meal.

# Connectivity

### Mobile Phones

Like most EU countries, the UK uses the GSM mobile service. This means that visitors from the EU should have no problem using their mobile phones, when visiting the UK. If visiting from the USA, Canada, Japan, India, Brazil or South Korea, you should check with your service provider about compatibility and roaming fees. The US service providers Sprint, Verizon and U.S. Cellular employ the CDMA network, which is not compatible with the UK's phone networks. Even if your phone does use the GSM service, you will still incur extra costs, if using your phone in the UK. For European visitors the rates will vary from 28p per minute for voice calls and 58p per megabyte for data. The alternative option would be to purchase a UK sim card to use during your stay in the UK. It is relatively easy to get a SIM card, though. No proof of identification or address details will be required and the SIM card itself is often free, when combined with a top-up package.

The UK has four mobile networks. They are Vodafone, O2, Three (3) and EE (Everything Everywhere), the latter of which grew from a merger between Orange and T-Mobile. All of these do offer pay-as-you-go packages that are tailor made for visitors. Through EE, you will enjoy access to a fast and efficient 4G network, as well as 3G and 2G coverage. There is a whole range of pay as you go products, which are still part of the Orange brand. These have been named after different animals, each with a different set of rewards. The dolphin package, which includes free internet and free texts will seem ideal to most tech savvy travellers. The canary plan offers free calls, texts and photo messages, while the raccoon offers the lowest call rate. Also through EE, you can choose from three different package deals, starting from as little as £1 and choose whether to favour data or call time.

With the Three packages, you will get a free SIM with the All-in-One package of £10. Your rewards will include a mix of 500Mb data, 3000 texts and 100 minutes calltime. It is valid for 30 days. Through the O2 network, you can get a free SIM card, when you choose from a selection of different top-up packages, priced from £10. As a service provider, O2 also offers users an international SIM card, which will enable you to call and text

## STRATFORD-UPON-AVON TRAVEL GUIDE

landline as well as mobile numbers in over 200 countries. With Vodafone, you can choose between a mixed top-up package that adds the reward of data to the benefit of voice calls and data only SIM card offer. The packages start at £10.

Alternately, you could also explore the various offers from a range of virtual suppliers, which include Virgin Mobile, Lebara Mobile, Lycamobile, Post Office Mobile and Vectone Mobile. Virtual Packages are also available through the retailers Tesco and ASDA.

**Dialling Code**

The international dialling code for the UK is +44.

**Emergency Numbers**

General Emergency: 999
(The European Union General emergency number of 112 can also be accessed in the UK. Calls will be answered by 999 operators)
National Health Service (NHS): 111
Police (non-emergency): 101

# STRATFORD-UPON-AVON TRAVEL GUIDE

MasterCard: 0800 056 0572

Visa: 0800 015 0401

## General Information

**Public Holidays**

1 January: New Year's Day (if New Year's Day falls on a Saturday or Sunday, the 2nd or 3rd of January may also be declared a public holiday).

17 March: St Patrick's Day (Northern Ireland only)

March/April: Good Friday

March/April: Easter Monday

First Monday in May: May Day Bank Holiday

Last Monday in May: Spring Bank Holiday

12 July: Battle of the Boyne/Orangemen's Day (North Ireland only)

First Monday of August: Summer Bank Holiday (Scotland only)

Last Monday of August: Summer Bank Holiday (everywhere in the UK, except Scotland)

30 November: St Andrew's Day (Scotland only)

25 December: Christmas Day

26 December: Boxing Day

# STRATFORD-UPON-AVON TRAVEL GUIDE

(if Christmas Day or Boxing Day falls on a Saturday or Sunday, 27 and/or 28 December may also be declared a public holiday)

## Time Zone

The UK falls in the Western European Time Zone. This can be calculated as Greenwich Mean Time/Co-ordinated Universal Time (GMT/UTC) 0 in winter and +1 in summer for British Summer Time.

## Daylight Savings Time

Clocks are set forward one hour at 01.00am on the last Sunday of March and set back one hour at 02.00am on the last Sunday of October for Daylight Savings Time.

## School Holidays

In the UK, school holidays are determined by city or regional authorities. This means that it could vary from town to town, but general guidelines are followed. There are short breaks to coincide with Christmas and Easter, as well as short mid terms for winter (in February), summer (around June) and autumn (in

# STRATFORD-UPON-AVON TRAVEL GUIDE

October). A longer summer holiday at the end of the academic year lasts from mid July to the end of August.

## Trading Hours

For large shops, trading hours will depend on location. There are outlets for large supermarket chains such as Asda and Tesco that are open round the clock on weekdays or may trade from 6am to 11pm. In England and Wales, the regulations on Sunday trading are set according the size of the shop. While there are no restrictions on shops less than 280 square meters, shops above that size are restricted to 6 hours trading on Sundays and no trading on Christmas or Easter Sunday. Post office trading hours vary according to region and branch. Most post offices are open 7 days a week, but hours may differ according to location.

In Scotland, the trading hours for most shops are from 9am to 5pm, Monday to Saturdays. In larger towns, urban city areas and villages frequented by tourists, many shops will elect to trade on Sundays as well. Some rural shops will however close at 1am on a weekday, which would usually be Wednesday or Thursday. Some shops have introduced late trading hours on Thursdays and longer trading hours may also apply in the summer months and in the run-up to Christmas. On the Scottish

## STRATFORD-UPON-AVON TRAVEL GUIDE

islands of Lewis, Harris and North Uist, all shops will be closed on a Sunday.

### Driving Policy

In the UK, driving is on the left side of the road. Both front and rear passengers must wear seat belts. If travelling with children, they must be accommodated with an age-appropriate child seat. With rental cars, it is advisable to make prior arrangements for this when you arrange your booking. If stopped by the police, you may be asked for your driver's licence, insurance certificate and MOT certificate, which must be rendered within 7 days. Driving without insurance could result in the confiscation of your vehicle.

In urban and residential areas, the speed limit for all types of vehicles is 48km per hour. On motorways and dual carriageways, cars, motorcycles and motor homes less than 3.05 tonnes are allowed to drive up to 112km per hour. On a single carriageway, this drops to 96km per hour. For motorhomes above 3.05 tonnes and vehicles towing caravans or trailers, the speed limit is 80km for single carriageways and 96km for dual carriageways and motorways. Local speed limits may vary. The alcohol limit for drivers is 35mg per 100ml of breath in England

and Wales and 22mg per 100ml of breath in Scotland (or 80mg and 50mg respectively per 100ml of blood).

**Drinking Policy**

The legal age for buying alcohol in the UK is 18. Young persons of 16 to 17 may drink a single beer, cider or glass of wine in a pub, provided they are in the company of an adult. From the age of 14, persons can enter a pub unaccompanied to enjoy a meal and children are allowed in pubs with their parents until 9pm. For buying alcohol at an off-license, you will need to be over 21 and may be asked to provide identification.

**Smoking Policy**

In the UK, smoking is prohibited in public buildings, all enclosed spaces and on public transport. Smoking is also prohibited at bus shelters. The law also states that 'no smoking' signage must be displayed clearly within all premises covered by the legislation. The only exceptions are rooms specifically designated as smoking rooms.

# STRATFORD-UPON-AVON TRAVEL GUIDE

## Electricity

Electricity: 230 volts

Frequency: 50 Hz

The UK's electricity sockets are compatible with the Type G plugs, a plug that features three rectangular pins or prongs, arranged in a triangular shape. They are incompatible with the two pronged Type C plugs commonly used on the European continent, as UK sockets are shuttered and will not open without the insertion of the third "earth" pin. If travelling from the USA, you will need a power converter or transformer to convert the voltage from 230 to 110, to avoid damage to your appliances. The latest models of certain types of camcorders, cell phones and digital cameras are dual-voltage, which means that they were manufactured with a built in converter, but you will have to check with your dealer about that.

## Food & Drink

England gave the world one of its favourite breakfast, the Full English, a hearty feast of bacon eggs, sausage, fried mushroom and grilled tomato. In the UK, this signature dish is incomplete without a helping of baked beans. In Scotland, you can expect to see black pudding or Lorne sausage added to the ensemble, while the Welsh often throw in some cockles or Laverbread.

# STRATFORD-UPON-AVON TRAVEL GUIDE

For simple, basic meals, you cannot go wrong with traditional pub fare. All round favourites include the beef pie, shepherd's pie, bangers and mash and toasted sandwiches. Fish and chips, served in a rolled up sheet of newsprint, is another firm favourite. For Sunday roast, expect an elaborate spread of roasted meat, roasted potatoes, vegetables and Yorkshire pudding. The national dish of Scotland is, of course, Haggis - sheep's offal which is seasoned and boiled in a sheep's stomach. This dish rises to prominence on Burns Night (25 January), when the birthday of the poet Robert Burns is celebrated. Burns wrote 'Address to a Haggis'. The influence of immigrants to the UK has led to kosher haggis (which is 100 percent free of pork products) and an Indian variant, Haggis pakora, said to have originated from the Sikh community. The synergy of Anglo-Indian cuisine also gave rise to popular dishes such as Chicken Tikka Masala and Kedgeree.

The neighbourhood pub is an integral part of social life in the UK and Britain is known for its dark ale, also referred to as bitter. Currently, the most popular beer in the UK is Carling, a Canadian import which has available in the British Isles since the 1980s. Foster's Lager, the second most popular beer in the UK, is brewed by Scottish & Newcastle, the largest brewery in Britain. For a highly rated local brew, raise a mug of award-winning Fuller's beer. The brewery was established early in the 1800s and produces London Pride, London Porter and Chiswick

# STRATFORD-UPON-AVON TRAVEL GUIDE

Bitter, to name just a few. A popular brand from neighbouring Ireland is Guinness. Along with Indian curries, the market share of Indian beer brands like Jaipur or Cobra beer has grown in recent years. Kent has developed as an emergent wine producer.

On the non-alcoholic side, you can hardly beat tea for popularity. The English like to brew it strong and serve it in a warmed china teapot with generous amounts of milk. Tea is served at 11am and 4pm. Afternoon tea is often accompanied with light snacks, such as freshly baked scones or cucumber sandwiches. High tea, served a little later at 6pm, can be regarded as a meal. A mixture of sweet and savoury treats such as cakes, scones, crumpets, cheese or poached egg on toast, cold meats and pickles. The custom of High Tea goes back to the days when dinner was the midday meal. These days, it is often replaced by supper.

Scotland is known for producing some of the world's finest whiskies. Its industry goes back at least 500 years. One of Scotland's best selling single malt whisky is produced by the famous Glenmorangie distillery in the Highlands. Chivas Brothers, who once supplied whisky by royal warrant to Queen Victoria's Scottish household, produce Chivas Regal, one of the best known blended whiskies of Scotland. The Famous Grouse, which is based at Glenturret near the Highlands town of Crieff, produces several excellent examples of blended grain whiskies.

# STRATFORD-UPON-AVON TRAVEL GUIDE

Bell's Whisky is one of the top selling whiskies in the UK and Europe. Other well known Scottish whisky brands include Old Pulteney, Glen Elgin, Tamdhu (a Speyside distillery that produces single malt), Balvenie, Bunnahabhain, Macallan, Aberlour, Bowmore, the award-winning Ballantine and Grant's whisky, from a distillery that has been run by the same family for five generations. Another proudly Scottish drink is Drambuie, the first liqueur stocked by the House of Lords. According to legend, its recipe was originally gifted to the MacKinnon clan by Bonnie Prince Charlie.

**Events**

**Sports**

Horse racing is often called the sport of kings and has enjoyed the support of the British aristocracy for centuries. Here you can expect to rub shoulders with high society and several races go back to the 1700s. The Cheltenham Festival is usually on or near St Patrick's Day and now comprises a four day event of 27 races. The Grand National takes place in Liverpool in April. With prize money of £1 million, this challenging event is Europe's richest steeplechase. A Scottish equivalent of the Grand National takes place in Ayr in the same month. There is

## STRATFORD-UPON-AVON TRAVEL GUIDE

also a Welsh Grand National, which now takes place in the winter at Chepstow. A past winner of Welsh event was none other than the author Dick Francis. Other important horse races are the Guineas at Newmarket (April/May), the Epsom Oaks and the Epsom Derby (first Saturday of June) and the St Leger Stakes, which takes place in Doncaster in September. One of the annual highlights is Royal Ascot week, traditionally attended by the British Royal Family. This takes place in June at Berkshire. There is a strict dress code and access to the Royal Enclosure is limited, especially for first timers. Fortunately, you will be able to view the the arrival of the monarch in a horse drawn carriage with a full royal procession at the start of the day. Another high profile equestrian event is the St Regis International Polo Cup, which takes place in May at Cowdray Park.

Wimbledon, one of the world's top tennis tournaments, takes place in London from last week of June, through to the first half of July. If you are a golfing enthusiast, do not miss the British Open, scheduled for July at Royal Troon in South Ayrshire, Scotland. The event, which has been played since 1860, is the world's oldest golf tournament. A highlight in motorcycle racing is the Manx Grand Prix, which usually takes place in August or September and serves as a great testing ground for future talent. The British Grand Prix takes place at Silverstone in Northamptonshire. A sporting event that occupies a special

## STRATFORD-UPON-AVON TRAVEL GUIDE

place in popular culture is the annual boat race that usually takes place in April between the university teams of Oxford and Cambridge. The tradition goes back to 1829 and draws large numbers of spectators to watch from the banks of the Thames. The FA Cup final, which is played at Wembley Stadium in May, is a must for soccer fans. As a sports event, the London Marathon is over 100 years old and draws entries from around the world to claim its prize money of a million pounds. Keen athletes will only have a brief window period of less than a week to submit their entries. Selection is by random ballot. The 42km race takes place in April.

### Cultural

If you want to brush shoulders with some of your favourite authors or get the chance to pitch to a British publisher or agent, you dare not miss the London Book Fair. The event takes place in April and includes talks, panel discussions and exhibitions by a large and diverse selection of publishing role players. The London Art Fair happens in January and features discussions, tours and performances. For comic geeks there are several annual events in the UK to look forward to. The CAPTION comic convention in Oxford, which goes back to the early 1990s, is a must if you want to show your support to Britain's

## STRATFORD-UPON-AVON TRAVEL GUIDE

small presses. There is a Scottish Comic Con that takes place in the Edinburgh International Conference Center in April and a Welsh Comic Con, also in April, at Wrexham. The MCM London Comic Con happens over the last weekends of May and October, and covers anime, manga, cosplay, gaming and science fiction in general. The UK's calendar of film festivals clearly shows its cultural diversity. The oldest events are the London Film Festival (October) and the Leeds Film Festival (November). There are also large events in Manchester and Cambridge. The high-profile Encounters festival for shorts and animated films takes place each September in Bristol.

History fans can immerse themselves in the thrills and delights of the Glastonbury Medieval Fayre, which takes place in April and includes stalls, jousting and minstrels. The Tewkesbury Medieval Festival takes place in summer and its key event is the re-enactment of the Battle of Tewkesbury.

Edinburgh has an annual International Film Festival that takes place in June. The city also hosts a broader cultural festival that takes place in August. The Edinburgh International Festival is a three week event that features a packed programme of music, theatre, dance and opera, as well as talks and workshops. The Royal Highland show takes place in June and features agricultural events as well as show jumping. If you want to experience the massing of Scottish pipers, one good opportunity is the Braemar Gathering, an event that takes place on the first Saturday in September and is usually attended by the Royal family. Its roots go back 900 years. Over the spring and summer seasons, you can attend numerous Highland Games, which feature Scottish piping, as well as traditional sports such as hammer throw and tug of war. For Scottish folk dancing, attend the Cowal Highland Gathering, which takes place towards the end of August.

**Websites of Interest**

http://www.visitbritain.com
http://www.myguidebritain.com/
http://wikitravel.org/en/United_Kingdom
http://www.english-heritage.org.uk/
http://www.celticcastles.com/
http://www.tourist-information-uk.com/

**Travel Apps**

If you are planning to use public transport around the UK, get Journey Pro to help make the best connections.
https://itunes.apple.com/gb/app/journey-pro-london-uk-by-navitime/id388628933

## **STRATFORD-UPON-AVON TRAVEL GUIDE**

The Around Me app will help you to orient, if you are looking for the nearest ATM, gas station or other convenience services. http://www.aroundmeapp.com/

If you are worried about missing out on a must-see attraction in a particular area, use the National Trust's app to check out the UK's natural and historical treasures.

http://www.nationaltrust.org.uk/features/app-privacy-policy

Printed in Great Britain
by Amazon